FROM the WORKHOUSE and BACK

The Life and Times

of

Thomas Dobson

1840 to 1917

Margaret Hart

Also by this author

Ten Men   ISBN-978-1-4717-7529-1

The Ribbons of Life   ISBN 978-0-244-37717-5

For my children

Richard, Sally-Ann,

Andrew and Anna-Marie

With love.

Dedication

This book is dedicated to the memory of the Thomas Dobson, my paternal great grandfather. I am the granddaughter of his last child, Elizabeth Dobson, through her marriage to Walter Bates.

Preface

The enforced lockdown during the Covid pandemic in 2021 gave me a year in which to focus my attention on the life of Thomas Dobson. He was a man who rose from humble beginnings to find his place in the hubbub of Victorian life in the garrison city of Canterbury in Kent.

Through my research I have come to a better understanding of this man who was, I believe, essentially a kind man who was fiercely protective of his family. He worked hard to support those he cared for and, despite his love of a drink or two, held a responsible position as a Master Baker in his local community. Writing this book has given me the privilege of getting to know him better and I am enriched by that knowledge.

Throughout the book I have tried to be as accurate as possible in stating facts and have double checked information where possible. However, Thomas had a very large family and the same names are often found in several generations. I apologise in advance for any unintentional errors or omissions.

Content

Chapter 1: The Workhouse.......................... 1

Chapter 2: The Brickfields........................ 13

Chapter 3: Elizabeth Dobson 21

Chapter 4: The Bakery............................. 27

Chapter 5: Married Life 35

Chapter 6: The Family............................. 55

Chapter 7: Old Age 73

Endnote 81

Canterbury Cemetery Records.................... 83

References and Acknowledgements 85

Postscript 87

Chapter One

The Workhouse

Thomas Dobson came into the world in November 1840 as an illegitimate baby. There was no rejoicing and delight at his arrival, but rather the shame and alienation of an unmarried mother who would have been shunned by society.

Thomas' mother, *Elizabeth*, was born to Charles Dobson and Elizabeth Smith in April 1814 in the small village of Broad Oak on the outskirts of Canterbury. When her parents were married, Elizabeth's mother was just sixteen and already pregnant. Elizabeth was the second child of a family of four siblings. Her father was a blacksmith who would have served a journeyman apprenticeship in his trade before starting out on his own. In the 1800's blacksmiths were among the most prosperous members of their small town or village. Charles would have spent most of his time in the forge. He would have been busy keeping the fire alight and melting down metal to be hammered it into essential tools, such as nails, farm implements and horse shoes for the people of the village. On occasions Elizabeth's father would have travelled out to farms in the surrounding areas to shoe horses. Blacksmiths were known for their size and strength which developed from the repeated hammering of the metal. Due to their particular calling, blacksmiths were often consulted as dentists, doctors, undertakers, vets and horse dealers.

At some time in her early life Elizabeth's family moved about half a mile away to Milton. This was a market town and parish adjoined to Sittingbourne and located by a branch of the Swale River. It had four wharfs and its narrow streets, lined with timber framed houses, were mostly inhabited by seafaring persons who were fishermen and oyster dredgers. The red sails of the fishermen's barges were a common sight, as were other barges carrying grain to the local mills. The area was very marshy and the stagnant water hosted mosquitoes which transmitted diseases, making it a bad area for health.

In 1826, when Elizabeth was twelve, her father died at the age of thirty five. This was a great blow to her mother, not least because she was left with four young children, the youngest being just being two years old. Having lost the support of her husband's income her mother would have been forced to rely on charity and the church to help them survive and escape destitution.

Elizabeth remained at home until her twenties when she started courting a labourer called Thomas. At the age of twenty three Elizabeth fell pregnant. Unlike her mother, whose partner had done the honourable thing and married her when she was with child, Elizabeth found herself on her own. Unmarried mothers in the 1800s faced social stigma and economic hardship. The woman was always considered to be at fault and many were turned away from the family home and sent to live elsewhere. More often than not, the only way for a mother and child to survive was to be separated. This meant babies being placed in a foundling hospital or taken by 'baby farmers'. Many babies were left abandoned to die by their desperate mothers. The Bastardy Clause of 1834 absolved fathers of responsibility for children born outside of wedlock. Mothers were made solely responsible for illegitimate children until they reached the age of sixteen. The Clause was introduced with the purpose of making the consequences of having to go into a workhouse sufficiently unattractive to deter women from risking extra-marital pregnancy.

On the 15th February 1837 Elizabeth gave birth to a son called Alfred. Three years later, at the beginning of November 1840, she gave birth to a second son called Thomas who was baptised on the 8th November in the Holy Trinity Church in Milton. Both the boys took Elizabeth's surname, so we do not know the family name of the father. What is certain though is that by this time Elizabeth was still living with a labourer by the name of Thomas. The family had managed to scrape by until Elizabeth gave birth for the second time, after which Thomas found himself out of work and unable to support them. The pair must have been in utter despair when they made the painful decision that they had no option but to seek help in the workhouse. The family unit was admitted into the Faversham Union Workhouse in December 1840. Families were admitted into the workhouse serving the parish where the head of the household had been born.

Thomas was recorded as being *'an able bodied labourer who had fallen on hard times'* and the reason given for their request for help was that *'they had two bastard children and no means of support.'* From this workhouse information it is clear that the couple were living together, but unmarried. This was not a common practice at the time, as reputation was the key to everything. However, the New Poor Law of 1834 did not see it as the responsibility of a man to be the bread winner. This law was based on the belief that if a man could not support his family, he should not marry, and if a woman could not find a husband who earned enough she must support herself and her children by earning wages. As Elizabeth's children were termed 'bastards', she was no longer eligible for outside relief and had no option but to enter the workhouse. The law aimed to deter working-class men from marrying by withdrawing state allowances for children and, as was the case here, forcing entire families into the workhouse to receive any form of relief.

The 1841 census shows that, at the time that the family were in the workhouse, there were three inmates named Thomas there at the same time. Two of these men were in their seventies, but the third was aged fifty. His name was Thomas Pierson and the records show that he was an agricultural worker. It would seem probable that this man was, in fact, Thomas' father although that can never be proved.

The formidable Faversham workhouse was opened on a cold January morning in 1836. It had a capacity for 450 inmates who were admitted from the surrounding parishes. The building was erected in a courtyard style with outer buildings surrounding a large inner space. Only four privies were allowed in a house of this size. The cost of the workhouse was paid for by the taxes of the middle and upper classes in each town. These people were suspicious that they were paying the poor to be lazy and avoid work. To combat this view conditions in workhouses were harsh and deliberately so in order that only people who desperately needed help would ask for it. Nothing lax or homely was to be permitted in the new union workhouses. Orders were given that the living conditions inside the workhouse should be less eligible than those of the poorest independent labourer outside.

A Board of some twenty, male Governors was appointed to oversee the day to day running of the workhouse and to ensure that orders and regulations sent by the Poor Law Commissioners in London were followed. In 1840 the Master and Matron of the workhouse were a John Pringuer and his wife Rebecca. John had first set up business in Canterbury as a glover. The job of this pair was not to be envied. They were held responsible for anything untoward that happened in the workhouse and whatever bad happened was blamed on them. Several workhouse masters were found to be brutal and drunken. They were often chosen for the job having previously been soldiers and used to instilling discipline. In 1841 the Guardians wanted to know why so many Faversham inmates were sent to prison compared with other neighbouring union workhouses. Pringuer said he could not give a reason. The Guardians decided that it was because he had, on occasion, shown harshness of manner and told him in future to '*be kind, but at the same time firm.*'

Rules in the workhouse were strict and could be harsh. Talking was forbidden at mealtimes (until 1842) and any disobedience, such as refusal to work, or uttering obscenities, brought the consequence of a visit to the punishment room and a cut in rations. A repeated offence meant a visit to the magistrate and probably twenty one days in prison.

In 1840 a girl of twenty one was given twenty four hours in the '*bridewell*' (place of correction) for being 'very saucy' when reprimanded. Four girls aged between seventeen and eighteen were sent for trial for destroying a bed rug '*on purpose to go to gaol.*'

Thomas and Elizabeth entered the workhouse through the single entrance that was guarded by a porter by the name of James Partis. It was his job to man the gate, locking up at night and unlocking in the morning. The family was immediately split up.

Thomas was sent into the segregated men's quarters and Elizabeth and the children to the women's quarters. The couple most likely never saw one another again. As Thomas was described as a member of the *'able bodied poor'* he would have been set to work in gainful employment, which would have kept him off the streets and enabled him to contribute to his keep.

Prior to formal admission, Elizabeth and her two children were put into the receiving ward where they were checked for their state of health and given a cleansing with an insect-killer. Their clothes were taken away, fumigated and stored ready for their release. Elizabeth was then issued with workhouse clothes and boots. Following this Elizabeth had to go before the weekly meeting of the Board of Guardians to justify her need for support. At the end of a gruelling cross questioning, Elizabeth was devastated to learn that Albert, aged three, was not going to be admitted and was to be removed from the workhouse by order of the Board. Arrangements were made for little Albert to be sent to Milton to live with his maternal grandmother, Elizabeth Dobson/nee Smith b.1796. On 18 Dec 1840, after spending eight days in the workhouse, the three year old Alfred left his mother behind and would not live with her again for the rest of his life.

On her admission into the workhouse, Elizabeth was allowed to keep baby Thomas with her. She was then taken to the mother and baby ward. The rooms were small and stuffy, as there were no windows on the outside walls. The dormitories were designed to be occupied by eight paupers (of the same sex) sharing four double beds. There was not a single trained nurse in the workhouse and those in need were cared for by female inmates, who most likely could not read and were often drunk. Commonly prescribed spirits, such as brandy, more often than not did not reach the patient for whom they were intended.

Young Thomas was one month old when he was taken to the workhouse and he spent the first year and seven months of his early childhood living there. He most likely shared the same bed as his mother in the dormitory ward. Children were allowed to stay with their mother until the age of two. After this they were put into the nursery ward and the mothers were put to hard and thankless tasks as servants in order to help pay for their food and accommodation. As a pauper, Elizabeth was not allowed out of the workhouse without permission. Short term absences were granted for exceptional circumstances, such as visiting a sick or dying relative. Inmates were allowed to discharge themselves by giving a period of notice of twenty four hours.

In winter the rising bell was rung at seven. An hour was then allowed for washing, prayers and breakfast and following this the inmates worked until midday. They were allowed half an hour for dinner and then work was resumed until six. Supper and prayers followed and all inmates were in bed by eight o'clock at night. In summer the paupers were woken at five and so had to work an hour longer. Elizabeth may have been put to laundry work, mending, sewing or cleaning.

Food in the workhouse was frugal. For breakfast they had gruel and a hunk of bread. The bread was made from cheap flour and not the best. There were many complaints about its texture and flavour. Dinner was usually a small piece of cheese with a slightly larger piece of bread than at breakfast. The highlight of the menu was the two days a week when the inmates were given a piece of meat or bacon with vegetables. Supper was cheese and bread again. In 1840 the cheese supplied to the Faversham workhouse came from Redman Brown and it was described as '*very bad and not at all the quality contracted for.*' His supply of butter was also reported to be of an inferior quality. Complaints from the paupers were simply ignored by the Board.

Once Elizabeth had finished nursing her child, the workhouse authorities found a job for her in the outside world. She was sent some sixteen miles away to become a servant in the Bell Inn in Canterbury, which had just come under new management. The position would have been granted on the condition that Elizabeth went as a single woman with no ties. In addition the workhouse authorities would have expected her to start to contribute to her son's upkeep. Once again Elizabeth turned to her mother for support and she and baby Thomas were discharged from the workhouse on 6th July 1842.

Thomas was just one year and eight months old when he started the next chapter of his life with his widowed maternal grandmother. Elizabeth senior was, by now, fifty two years old. She lived in Valenciennes, near to the High Street in Milton. Her eldest child, Charles, had already married and left home, but he lived right next door to her with his young family. When Thomas went to live with his grandmother his brother Alfred was four years old and two of his uncles were still living at home.

For the next twelve years Thomas enjoyed a family life where he had his brother and cousins to play with and a grandmother and three uncles to watch over him. His mother most likely came back from Canterbury to visit him when she was able, although this would not have been very often as her release from work would have been very limited.

It is unlikely that Thomas learned to read and write. There were women who earned a living as school mistresses in the area, but they charged for their services and his grandmother could not have afforded to pay the fees. There was a school in the Court House which catered for nine or ten poor boys on charity, but it is unlikely that Thomas was one of the lucky ones. The compulsory Elementary Education Act was not introduced until 1870.

Childhood was brief in those days, but nevertheless children did play out in the street in front of their houses. Thomas would have spent time with his cousin Charles who lived next door and was born in the same year as him. When the boys were seven years old cousin Charles became unwell. Their grandmother Elizabeth did all she could to help. For two days she watched helplessly as Charles struggled for breath, but sadly on the 2 December 1847 he died of the croup. This was a cruel and distressing way to die and must have been an agonising experience for his grandmother Elizabeth who was present at the time of his death. For Thomas this would be his first experience of the death of a close relative and a sobering time, but unfortunately more was to follow.

In general the health of the nation was in a poor condition during the Victorian Age and doctors had little medical knowledge as to the causes of many ailments. Without the help of antibiotics many people died, often at a young age. The biggest killer of the mid-nineteenth century was a third cholera outbreak, which probably arrived on ships bringing imports from China.

Although a great number of people in the Milton area were involved in the fishing industry, the young Thomas grew up in a brick making family and this would influence the next chapter of his life.

Chapter Two

The Brickfields

Milton, near Sittingbourne, was a market town and fishing port. It was also in the region of one of the largest brick manufacturers in the area, as it was situated next to the parish of Murston. Both parishes lay either side of the River Medway and both parishes were bounded by the coast of the Swale. The ever growing expansion of London meant that bricks were in high demand and the local soil of the area was ideal for the purpose. Large areas of the marshland were used for gravel extraction, which was an essential part of the brick making process. Milton's access to the river Medway also provided the ideal way to transport the bricks to the city. Specially adapted barges carried the finished bricks to London and returned with the waste of ash and clinker from London's fireplaces, which was another essential brick making ingredient.

The brickfields were dangerous and dirty places to work, but they provided employment for many of the poor labourers living in cottages in the narrow streets of the area. Brick workers were known to be rough, tough men. They often quarrelled and fought and most were heavy drinkers.

Two of Elizabeth Dobson's sons were such labourers. There was Thomas, aged twenty four, and Frederick, aged eighteen, who were working in the brickfields when young Thomas left the workhouse and went to live with them. Every morning at five o'clock Thomas would be woken by his uncles getting up and readying themselves for their walk to work. He would not see them again until seven or eight at night when they made their weary way home.

When Thomas was eight years old, he witnessed another family tragedy when his Uncle Frederick died. Frederick had suffered from declining health for some time. He found long days in the brickfields particularly gruelling and was often confined to his bed. On 24 August 1848, Frederick died at the age twenty four. His mother, Elizabeth, nursed him to the end and was at his bedside when he died. Frederick died of consumption, now better known as tuberculosis. This was a common disease of the poor which was linked with overcrowding and malnutrition. The duration of active tuberculosis from onset to death was approximately three years. There was no known cure for the disease, which would have left Frederick with chest pains, fever, night sweats, severe weight loss and a prolonged cough.

Apart from the grief of losing a son, Elizabeth also found that there was now only one son left to bring in a weekly wage. It then became a necessity that Thomas be sent out to work at the age of nine years. He followed his uncles into the brickfields. Child labour in this period was common among the poor and they were exploited and badly treated. The 1844 Child Labour Act had just come into force making it illegal for children under the age of thirteen to work more than six hours a day. This was small consolation for a young boy who was expected to work hard for very little pay in what were taxing and sometimes dangerous conditions.

The Murston Brickfields

The men worked in brick making gangs of six to eight individuals, each with their own specific job. It was common for members of the same family to work in the same gang and there was often great camaraderie between the gangs. Thomas' uncle was a close friend of the brick maker William Ager. No doubt this was a friendship made through work and the men probably worked in the same team. William and his wife Elizabeth did not have any children of their own, but they were fond of Thomas. The 1851 census records the young ten year old Thomas visiting them. William also had a young nephew called John Ager, who was a few years older than Thomas, and they would also have been friends.

Grown men were expected to work for eight and a half hours six days a week. The brick making process was heavily influenced by the weather. In winter the clay had first to be dug out of the ground by hand. These workers could routinely shovel up to 20 tons of earth per day from below their feet to above their heads. This was an enormous physical effort that required great strength, stamina and robust good health. The earth was then built into piles known as Kerfs which were about three feet high and twenty feet square. Chalk, cinders and other rubbish was then mixed in and the pile was left to weather. The resulting mixture was then sent to a wash mill where it was mixed with water to combine the ingredients to make them suitably pliant for use. This work was carried out by horses attached to a frame by a yolk and harness that walked in circles rotating the harrows. Following this, the partly prepared brick earth was removed and stored under water until needed.

In spring the process of making the bricks began in earnest. At this point the mixture was taken to the Pug-Mill, where again a horse was attached to a yoke and walked in circles to operate cutting blades which mixed the mixture ready for use. As the lowest in the work chain, Thomas would have worked as a bearer. It would have been his job to carry wet clay from the pug mill to the brick makers table where it would have been shaped into bricks by the moulder. This work would have involved carrying very heavy loads and for a child would have been especially taxing.

After moulding, the bricks were moved in barrows to the drying racks. Thomas may well have undertaken this work as well. In this case it would have been his job to take moulded bricks and place them on their associated pallet where they were laid out to dry. Heavy rain stopped work and hot, dry weather dried out the bricks and also slowed down production. When the bricks were finally dried they were moved to the kilns by men called Crowders. It was their job to push loads of eighty bricks, weighing about four hundred pounds at a time, to be stacked in the kilns ready for firing. This part of the brick making process took two or three days resulting in obnoxious gases being released in to the air.

Thomas had been working in the brickfields for five years when the December of 1854 heralded another significant change in the Dobson family. Uncle Thomas had married and left home several years ago and now there were only Thomas and his brother Alfred living with their grandmother. During this time their grandmother had returned to work as a charwoman to make ends meet. Elizabeth was, in effect, a part time cleaner in the houses of others. However, she was not in good health. She had developed a tumour in her stomach. This made it very difficult for her to eat. For months she had suffered with heartburn and indigestion. She often felt sick and her lack of food resulted in weight loss. She developed a hard lump in her abdomen which the doctor was unable to do anything about. For seven months she suffered with exhaustion. Her son Thomas lived in Love Lane at the time and further down the lane there was living a young girl called Jane Simmons. Jane had come over from the island of Jersey looking for work. Thomas enlisted her help in looking after his mother until the end. Jane was present at Elizabeth's death on 9 December 1854 and left her mark as a witness on the death certificate.

The death of their grandmother left Thomas and his brother Alfred at a crossroad. They now both needed to find a new path for the future.

Alfred was seventeen at this time, but six months before he had signed up for ten years voluntary service in the Royal Navy following his upcoming eighteenth birthday. His service number was 13977. His registration papers record him as joining the ship Waterloo. HMS Waterloo (1833) was a 120-gun first rate ship of the Royal Navy, launched on 10th June 1833 at Chatham. At the time Alfred left home he was aged seventeen. His papers record that he was *'five feet three and quarter high, in robust health, with brown hair and grey eyes.'*

HMS Waterloo

Thomas was now fourteen years old. He had been working in the brickfields for some five years and his experience of life had taught him that the dirty, backbreaking toil of the field labourer was not for him. With the loss of his grandmother, his brother off to sea and his remaining uncle married and bringing up a family of his own, Thomas needed to plan his own future. His mother had carved out a new life for herself in Canterbury and, with her help, Thomas now set about looking for work in the big city.

Chapter Three

Elizabeth Dobson

Thomas' Mother

In 1842 when Elizabeth left the workhouse and moved to Canterbury she entered an ancient, oval shaped, walled garrison city crossed by two branches of the river Stour. The magnificent tower of the cathedral would have been the most striking thing for Elizabeth to see as she approached her new surroundings. She entered a city filled with people from all aspects of life, from the many wealthy clergymen serving the cathedral and living a secure life in its precincts, to the humble poor eking out an existence in the hovels of its narrow streets. At the time, Canterbury was a city filled with many beautiful and historic buildings, but, unfortunately, it was not a healthy place to live. There was no indoor sanitation and most of the effluent flowed into the River Stour and clogged it up. This led to the river flooding in the winter and breeding disease in the summer.

Elizabeth's destination was the High Street. This half a mile section of road was a busy through-way leading from London to Dover. Her new home was The Bell Inn at 15 High Street which had been built in 1803. It was advertised as '*a Stabling and Lock Up Coach House with omnibuses to all parts morning and evening, good will and aired beds*'. Elizabeth's employers were the licensed victuallers George and

Elizabeth Oakenfield, who had just taken over the running of the premises.

Elizabeth's new employers at the Bell Inn.

The Inn was in a thriving part of town and would have had a constant turnover of travellers seeking rest and shelter. George did not enjoy good health and after seven years at the Inn he died at the age of thirty five following a lingering illness. After his death, Elizabeth continued as a house servant to his widow and two young children.

There were numerous public houses in the city of Canterbury and drink was a huge social problem. This was not helped by the constant influx of soldiers from the Military Barracks, which also led to a rise in prostitution. Public houses were open until twelve o'clock at night and the constabulary were kept busy with many unruly incidents and petty thefts. As a servant Elizabeth would have had very little time for herself and would have been at the beck and call of her employers. She would, however, have come across visitors to the Bell. She may even have been serving drinks in the bar when she struck up a friendship with a man called William Nisbett.

William Nisbett had enjoyed a comfortable married life for ten years with his wife Elizabeth Newing. They had originally set up home in 33 Castle Row, where William had worked as a publican in The White House Inn. This public house was presumed to have been built on the ancient site of the long demolished church of St Mary-de-Castro. The beer cellars of the ancient building were once used as a temporary mortuary. The graveyard was situated in the adjourning plot and people working in the pub claimed to have seen ghosts and heard deathly moaning coming from next door.

William and his wife had eight girls, at least one of whom was born while he was living in the White House Inn, but sadly five of them died. This took a toll on his wife's health and William moved the family to 17 Abbotts Place which was located in the city centre. His wife's health continued to suffer and in April 1850, at the age of thirty four, she died. At this point William's unmarried sister moved into the house to help look after his three youngest children who were aged ten, six and two. William worked as a porter, which basically meant carrying and lifting work, so it may be that part of his job entailed taking and collecting beer barrels from the Bell public house where Elizabeth was working.

However they met, it was over the period of the next two years that William courted Elizabeth Dobson. William was in need of a wife to help with the children and Elizabeth was in need of a husband to take her out of service, and so their relationship blossomed. The couple were married in July 1852. Elizabeth was thirty four years old when she moved into the house at 17 Abbotts Place and became stepmother to William's girls. At the time that Elizabeth moved into the house there were still three of the girls living at home. Maria was eleven, Catherine was seven and Elizabeth was two. From having to leave her own two sons behind, Elizabeth now found herself surrounded by William's brood of little girls.

Elizabeth could now enjoy a stable family life. Her home in Abbotts Place was just behind King Street and close to Canterbury Cathedral. This meant that she was living in the centre of the city with easy access to the shops and the bustling life to be found there. This change in Elizabeth's fortunes ensured that she now had a secure base and a husband to provide for her.

Elizabeth had been married for two years when her mother died and left her two sons homeless. With Alfred signed up for a life in the navy, Elizabeth turned her attention to Thomas who was now fourteen and in need of a new home. The City of Canterbury was a busy and bustling place and, although jobs were menial and not very well paid, there were plenty of opportunities to be found.

Chapter Four

The Bakery

By the age of fourteen Thomas had experienced the pain of hardship and loss. His formative years had set the stage for the man he was to become as he arrived in Canterbury to start the next phase of his life.

Canterbury Cathedral

Thomas had secured a position as an apprentice in one of the many shops in a city where trade was brisk and willing workers always in demand. He had left the brickfields to become a journeyman baker in the home of the Master Baker, Thomas Tilbe and his wife Maria. Thomas was now indentured to the Tilbe family for the next seven years that it would take for him to achieve the official grade of 'baker'. His new home was the Bakers Shop at 39 Union Street which was on the corner of the Military Road which led up to the Canterbury Barracks.

Thomas worked long hours, but he was learning a trade which was going to prove more than useful to him. He had exchanged the cold, muddy, outdoor surroundings of the brickfields for the heat and floury surroundings of the bakery. A Victorian baker's life was a hard one. Daily work started at eleven or twelve at night with the making of the dough, after which the baker might then be able to get some sleep while the bread rose. After this he would work for ten, twelve, or even fourteen hours a day in an extremely hot environment. In London many bakers rarely lived past the age of forty two. Apart from the unsociable hours, Thomas had to get used to the constant particles of flour which floated in the air and were known to cause lung problems among bakers. Thomas was, however, used to long hours and hard work and he began to thrive. In addition, his mother lived a few minutes away in a nearby street and their relationship also began to prosper.

Children were often apprenticed out from the workhouse to take up a trade, but by 1850 this system had started to fall by the wayside in the bakery trade due in one part to the Assizes of Bread. These early laws adjusted the weight of bread according to the price of wheat. The price of a loaf of bread remained the same, even if the weight of the bread altered. A bakers' livelihood depended on the availability and price of flour.

The Corn Laws of 1815 were introduced to limit the amount of foreign grain that could come into the country from abroad. This was done with the intention of protecting the profits of landowners and British farmers. This naturally led to shortages and high prices for grain, which badly affected the poor. Bakers were accused of adulterating their bread through the use of alum, lime, chalk or powdered bones to disguise the use of low grade flour and keep it white. With limited availability of flour, attempts to ensure a standard weight for loaves led to devious methods of weighing which inevitably cheated the customer. During this time the desirability of going into the bakery trade dwindled. In an effort to prevent any fraud in the system, the standard weight for loaves was abolished in 1822 and replaced with the requirement for every loaf to be weighed in front of the customer. This led to the practice of bakers adding a little extra piece of bread with the loaf to avoid being fined for selling an underweight loaf. This became known as 'a baker's dozen'.

In 1888 the National Association of Master Bakers and Confectioners was formed and examinations were introduced with the aim of promoting trade education. The exams consisted of two standards, one of which included a high scientific content and a written paper including ten questions.

In addition to the need to acquire a good supply of grain, bakers also required a large hot oven. In the 1800's the poor only had an iron pot suspended over an open fire with which to cook their food. This meant that many people resorted to taking their uncooked food to the bakery to be cooked in the baker's large oven. The affluent could afford their own coal fired, black range to cook their food.

January 1858 proved to be a pivotal point in Thomas' career. The baker Thomas Tilby died at the age of thirty three, leaving behind a pregnant wife. The baker's widow gave birth to a son two months later, and she still had four other children under ten to cater for. Thomas was eighteen at this point and half way through his apprenticeship. He helped with the running of the bakery shop for the widow Tilby and proved himself to be a conscientious and reliable worker. There was dough to kneed, heavy sacks of flour to be carried and a steady stream of customers to be attended to.

The following year, when Thomas was nineteen, he and his mother Elizabeth received some tragic news from the family in Milton. His Uncle Thomas (who had been a father figure to him) had died in an appalling accident while working in a brick making quarry. The death was reported by the Kentish Gazette on Tuesday 8 February 1859.

'SITTINGBOURNE FATAL ACCIDENT – *On Wednesday afternoon about four o'clock, an accident of a most painful nature happened to a man, named Thomas Dobson, in the vicinity of the town, by which he met with his death. The deceased, it appears, was at work, with other men, in a part of Mr. Huggens' brickfield, better known as the 'Dark Orchard,' and was engaged in removing the earth. In order to carry on their operation more expeditiously it is customary to undermine the ground, and the poor fellow, it seems, was thus employed, when the earth gave way, and he was buried underneath several tons falling upon him. He was extricated as soon as possible, but when found was a corpse, being crushed in a most fearful manner, several of his bones being broken and his bowels protruding. Information was at once given to the coroner, who arrived on the following morning and visited the spot where the sad occurrence took place. He, however, did not consider it necessary to hold any inquest, but suggested that more precaution should be taken in carrying on work similar to that in which the deceased was engaged. The unfortunate man, who resided in Love-lane, Milton, was 37 years of age, and he left a widow and three children.'*

This was devastating for the family and shattering news for his three girls who were fourteen, eleven and nine at the time. Thomas' death cast a very long shadow, throwing his widow Frances into a state of near destitution. She moved into a house in Sittingbourne High Street with John Ager (nephew of her late husband's best friend.) who was recorded as a lodger. However, the wagging tongues of the day claimed that Emily, the youngest of the children and obviously born before Thomas died, was actually fathered by John.

Frances and her daughter Emma were at odds at this difficult time and rumour and speculation seems to have fuelled the situation. It is no wonder that tension arose when Emma thought the 'lodger' was taking her late father's place. As times were still hard, Frances thought that her daughter should receive help from the parish for her upkeep. The East Kent Gazette of 11 Jan 1862 shows that Frances was called before the magistrate to explain her case.

Frances Dobson, of Milton, widow, was summoned to show cause why she should not contribute to the maintenance of her daughter, Emma Dobson, aged 15, who was chargeable to the parish of Sittingbourne. The defendant said she was in a state of utter destitution, and her daughter had behaved to her in a most ungrateful manner. It appeared, however, that the mother had acted in a very cruel way towards the girl and some disclosures were made concerning the woman that led to a well-merited censure from the bench as to her morals and mode of living. The bench decided that the case should stand over for a time.'

Frances eventually ended up alone in the Bayford brickfield cottages where she was a lodger and worked as a nurse to pay for her keep.

Meanwhile back in Canterbury, despite working hard in the bakery and having little time off work, Thomas still found the time see his mother Elizabeth. Through his visits with her, he got to know the three girls she was now stepmother to. The oldest of the girls was Maria who was the same age as him.

Maria and Thomas had both experienced difficult childhoods. Maria's mother had died when she was ten years old and for two years she had been brought up by her aunt, who was her father's unmarried sister. Maria was twelve years old when her father married Thomas' mother, which meant that Maria had now to adjust to a new mother figure in her life.

By the time Thomas had moved to Canterbury to become a journeyman baker, Maria had left home to take up work as a servant in the house of the Rev. Francis Smith from the church of St Peter and Holy Cross. Rev. Smith lived in a big house at 21 Green Court which was part of the monastery area outside of Canterbury Cathedral where all the important church dignitaries were housed. Maria was one of three servants in the house and she was employed as the cook along with a nurse and a housemaid. The Rev. Smith had a wife, seven children and three boarders living in the house. With so many mouths to feed Maria would have been as busy as Thomas in providing food for others. However, through Thomas' mother these two young people were drawn together and they continued to develop their friendship over the coming years.

In June 1861 after just nine years of marriage to Thomas' mother, William Nisbett died at the age of forty five. He left behind two daughters, Catherine, who was fourteen and Eliza, who was twelve. Thomas and Maria were now further bound together in support of their mother and the family - Thomas as a son, and Maria as a step daughter. During this time their bond became even closer and four months after her father's death, Maria found herself pregnant.

Chapter Five

Married Life

The death of William Nisbett proved to be a troubling time for Thomas. He now had his grieving, widowed mother and his pregnant sweetheart to support. As soon as signs of Maria's pregnancy began to show, she lost her job, as was the custom of the time. It is most likely that at this time Maria returned to her family home and the care of Thomas' mother, whilst Thomas himself started to search for new accommodation. The couple did not get married when Maria first became pregnant, possibly because the terms of Thomas' employment as a journeyman baker did not allow this and he had to wait until his apprenticeship came to an end. This fact may well have led to some bad feeling between Thomas and his employer Mrs Tilby.

Maria's baby was born in July 1862. She had a son, who was baptised Alfred Ernest on 7 September that year under the name of Dobson Nisbett. The baby was nine months old by the time the couple were able to marry on the 10th March 1863, following the calling of their banns at the end of 1862. Thomas and Maria were both twenty three when they married in the ancient, parish church of St Alphage, which was a two minute walk from the cathedral. It is interesting to note that a copy of their marriage certificate states Thomas' father as being 'Thomas Dobson – baker.' This obviously referred to him and not to his actual father whom he had never known and who, in any case, had long since vanished. The marriage certificate was witnessed by their married friends who lived further along King Street.

Thomas had lost no time in searching for a home for his family and they settled into family life at 30 King Street, which was close to Maria's previous home. King Street was situated in the shadow of the towering Canterbury Cathedral. It was a narrow street bordered on both sides by closely packed terrace houses, the front doors of which led on to the street via a step down on to the pavement. The Dobson's neighbours in King Street held a variety of different trades including a printer, organ builder, cabinet maker, shoe maker, painter, French polisher, needlewoman, tailor, photographer, baker, bricklayer, milliner, coachman, domestic servant, shoe binder, wheelwright, chimney sweep and licensed victuallers.

King Street Canterbury.

Meanwhile the bad feeling between Thomas and Mrs Tilby rumbled on. It finally raised its head nine months after the birth of his baby, when the following paragraph appeared in the Canterbury Journal and Farmers' Gazette on Saturday 24 October 1863.

'Mrs Tilby complained that on Friday evening as she was leaving the theatre, Mr. Dobson, a baker, residing in King Street, threatened to strike her. The bench sent for Mr Dobson, and he having promised not to insult the complainant again, he was dismissed.'

Three months later the dispute was still rankling.

23 January 1864 Canterbury Journal and Farmers' Gazette.

'Mr Dobson applied to the court under the following circumstances. He said that on Saturday last an announcement appeared in the Canterbury Journal to the effect that Mrs Tilbe of Union Street, had been confined of a son. That announcement was in-correct, and that Mrs Tilbe now charged him with inserting that announcement.

The Clerk.- But if you go to the newspaper office they will tell you who gave the authority for the insertion.

Mr Dobson and Mrs Tilbe had been to the office and obtained the announcement from there, and that it bore the name of Mrs Crow. He was not only charged with inserting the notice, but also with forging Mrs Crow's name.

In answer to the question from the bench, the applicant said he should be satisfied if Mrs Tilbe apologised to him. The Mayor advised the applicant to get a friend to call on Mrs Tilbe, and ask her to make an apology.'

If Mrs Tilbe had indeed refused to release Thomas from his apprenticeship in order that he could marry before his child was born, then he may well have held some resentment against her. His actions may have been his attempt to let her know what it was like to be regarded with distain by the local community as an unmarried mother. After all, as an illegitimate child himself, Thomas may well have been highly sensitive to the issue. He was a tough, working class man and experience had already taught him that he had to stand up for himself in life.

Clothing for the family was very much a case of 'hand me downs'. Many outfits would have been bought second hand and patched and mended to make them last as long as possible. When he was not working, Thomas wore trousers, shirt, a waistcoat and a flat cap. Maria wore a long skirt covered by a large apron tied at the waist. Her hair was always gathered up in a bun and often covered by a sheer hairnet to keep everything in place.

Before 1868 there was no drainage system in Canterbury and the stench from open privies could be almost overpowering, but that year saw work well underway with streets being dug up and drain pipes being laid. Unfortunately, the whole project was riddled with problems and sewage was still being discharged into the River Stour in 1871. There were many mouths to feed in the homes of the poor and not a lot of food to go round. Many poor people had been raising pigs in their back yard, but this caused varying degrees of squalor and a 'Nuisance Inspector' was appointed to record the number of offences he uncovered. In the narrow streets outside there were horses and carts going past as the people of the area went about their daily business. Night time did not provide any respite. The soldiers from the Barracks were always in evidence, as there were over two thousand men stationed there.

In order to try and reduce the huge numbers of soldiers suffering from venereal disease, a compulsory medical inspection of suspected prostitutes in garrison towns was ordered in 1869. An examination station was opened in Canterbury and plain clothed policemen came down from London to scour the streets for 'girls of the town'. Many girls refused to be examined and there were ugly scuffles in nearby streets. There was such an outcry from the local population that the act was repealed in 1883. Thomas certainly lived in colourful times.

The first few years of their married life was a happy time for Thomas and Maria. Babies came at a regular pace and filled the house with love and laughter, but in October 1866 a black cloud formed over the family. Little Alfred, their first born child, had been suffering from crippling abdominal pain. As his condition worsened, the pain became so bad that it was decided that an operation was necessary. He was taken into the Kent and Canterbury hospital where the surgery was performed. Unfortunately peritonitis was a major complication of this procedure and this is what Alfred died of shortly after his operation. He was just four years old.

Alfred's condition was caused by a build up of stones in the bladder. The condition was most commonly found in children under the age of ten and it was more likely to affect males. Drinking hard water carries a high risk of vesical calculus and it was known that the drinking water in Canterbury at the time was poor.

At this time of this tragedy, Marie and Thomas already had two other sons. Frederick who was two years old and Thomas junior aged one. In addition Maria was already pregnant again. She was delivered of a fourth son, named William, on the 4th April 1867, just six months after the death of her first born.

Childhood diseases such as small pox, whooping cough, measles and scarlet fever were rife in Thomas' time, in addition to the high number of cases of typhus caused by the unsanitary conditions. In one year alone one hundred and eighteen children under the age of five had died, many of them from the outbreak of cholera reported earlier in the year. The pain of losing young children was felt by many families.

Born in the Victorian era, both Thomas and Maria were used to poverty and hard work. They were members of the lower working class and, as such, their home was basic with an open fire and no running water. As their family grew this put more and more strain on the living accommodation and Thomas' need to put food into hungry mouths. His young children spilled out on to the street in front of the house where they could meet friends and play simple games together. The harsh experiences of his own early childhood contributed to Thomas becoming a loving husband and a protective father. He certainly stood up for his family whether it was verbally or, at times, with a little more vigour! Like many of his contemporaries his irascible outbursts were often fuelled by his drunkenness.

Thomas with his wife Maria and son Arthur - dressed in his Buffs uniform.

The figure in front is an unnamed grandson.

In 1865 Thomas found himself in trouble with the law once again. The Canterbury Journal and Farmers' Gazette recorded the following incident on the 13th June that year.

'*CHARGE OF ASSULT. Thomas Dobson, a baker of St Alphage, was charged with assaulting Richard Poole, also residing in St. Alphage, on Tuesday, the 2nd inst.*

Complainant said that on Tuesday evening last, he was quietly walking down St. Alphage towards home, and when he arrived as far as defendants house, outside of which was a vehicle, defendant pushed him against one of the walls, and would not allow him to pass. Defendant afterwards rushed at him and forced him against the house, and then complainant pushed him away. Defendant struck him on the head 5 or 6 times.

A young woman named Tomlin said she witnessed the whole affair. When complainant was going down the street, defendant was closing the door of the carriage that was standing in front of his house. Poole pushed Dobson away, and the latter then pushed Poole, who pushed defendant again. She did not see any blows struck on either side.

At the suggestion of Alderman Aria, the parties withdrew from Court to see if they could come to some amicable arrangement of the matter. When they returned Dobson said they were willing to divide the expenses between them, and the Magistrate therefore dismissed the case, complainant and defendant having to pay 4s 6p each.'

As the years passed the family continued to grow. Annie Maria arrived in Oct 1868. There was no new baby in 1870 and it is most likely that Maria miscarried.

Sometime in 1870, when the last of William Nisbett's daughters left home, Thomas' mother, Elizabeth, moved into her son's house at 30 King Street where she lived out the rest of her life. Thomas was now in the unusual position of having his mother, who was at the same time also his wife's stepmother and mother in law, living with them. With so many children to take care of Maria would surely have been grateful for another helping pair of hands as the babies kept coming.

Thomas had, by now, attained the title of Master Baker and was self employed. Achieving the title of Master Baker meant that he could set himself up as an independent baker who could either run his own business or hire out his services to others. At this time Thomas took in a seventeen year old servant named Joseph who was, in his turn, serving his apprenticeship under Thomas as a journeyman baker.

On 12 July 1870 the Kentish Gazette records another of Thomas' altercations.

'ASSAULT. George Betsworth was summoned for assaulting Thomas Dobson on Friday last. Thomas Dobson said that he had been on very friendly

terms with the defendant for the last 16 years, but lately he had observed a great coolness in his demeanour towards him. On Friday night, at about 11.30p.m. he was going home through King Street, when he saw defendant standing talking to another man. He went up to them and said to defendant, "Hallo, George, what's the matter with your temper, old fellow?" Defendant then said something about weight, and he would make him feel the weight, or something of that sort, and hit witness with his open hand knocking his hat off. Witness then remonstrated, and defendant struck him a heavy blow on the right jaw, which knocked him down insensible. Witness was not drunk at the time, nor did he scratch the defendant's face or pull his whiskers.

Emily Powell said that on Friday about 11.30 p.m. she saw defendant knock the prosecutor's hat across the road and then knock him down insensible.

Defendant stated that the cause of his ill will to the prosecutor was that he had kept back 6p which ought to have been given to him (defendant) for carrying a sack of flour. When the prosecutor came up to him he was quite drunk and did not take much knocking down. He only pushed him away.

The magistrates considered both parties wrong in the matter and was surprised that as the men had been good friends for so many years they could not have settled the dispute out of court; but as the result was proved they inflicted the nominal penalty of 1s. and costs.'

In March 1872 Maria had a son named Charles, who survived just long enough to be baptised on the 10 March and died in Oct

1872 aged six months. Following this sad period, Marie gave birth to Arthur Edward in Jan 1874, Frank in Jan 1876, Percival in Oct 1877, Elizabeth Mary in Jan 1880 and Alexander in March 1882. Baby Alexander was christened on the 18 May that year and was buried on the 25 July aged just four months. All of Maria's children had been born at home. She had the support of her step mother and the local midwife, but very little else. By the time she was forty one years of age, Maria had given birth to eleven children. Eight of whom were still living and three had died.

As Thomas became better known as a Master Baker, his standing in the local area began to grow and he began to take an interest in supporting the community. In April 1872 he was appointed joint overseer of the parish of St. Alphage and he was a staunch Conservative. Since medieval times, Canterbury had been entitled to return two Members of Parliament. Then, as now, there were two main political parties. The Conservative Party, whose colours were red, and the Whig Party, whose colours were blue. For many years there were electoral malpractices in the city as the two parties vied for power. Both sides did their best to bribe the electorate with 'colourmen' who carried the colours. These men were given sums of money to distribute to their voters, but there were instances of their 'embezzling' the money for their own use. The colourmen were also engaged at five shillings a day to join a procession which carried the colours of the party through the streets. They were preceded by a band playing rousing tunes and the candidate and friends after them. The colourmen followed up at the rear waving and protecting their colourful silk flags and banners. The proceedings could become very lively, especially if they encountered their opponents coming in the opposite direction or too many beers had been imbibed. Riots were known to break out and in some cases opponents were thrown into the River Stour.

Thomas was no stranger to these proceedings and was an active electoral supporter. As late as 1881 George Brown, a French Polisher and Cabinet Maker, who lived at 16 King Street, claimed that 'Dobson' had given him 10s. to ensure his vote. Shortly after this a general enquiry into the city's electoral proceedings was held. The result of the Commission's findings was that Canterbury was disenfranchised and ended up without a Member of Parliament for the next five and a half years.

There were still many soldiers from the garrison roaming the streets of the city and many of them frequented the public houses, which helped to keep the local constabulary in work. The Canterbury police force was formed in 1836 and its first police station was a disused abattoir in Crown Yard, Stour Street where a stable was converted into three cells. The force was ill disciplined and the men had so many public houses on their beat that they themselves were often drunk.

There were over one hundred public houses in Canterbury at the time and four of these were in King Street - The Crown and Anchor, The Military Tavern, the Prince of Wales with the Little Rose, which was situated on the corner. The Military Tavern was located directly opposite Thomas' house.

The Military Tavern

This establishment had its fair share of drunken incidents and brawls, often occurring late at night. Thomas and the landlord had an uneasy relationship and Thomas was not above being caught up in verbal altercations, especially if he was the worse for drink himself. One such incident occurred on 24th November 1885 when Thomas and his son Frederick, who was twenty one at the time, were involved in an argument at the Military Tavern. The Canterbury Journal and Kentish Times and Farmers Gazette recorded the following incident in the 12 December edition of the newspaper.

'ASSAULT *Thomas Dobson and Frederick Dobson, father and son, bakers, of King Street, were summoned for assaulting William Joslin, landlord of the Military Tavern, King Street, on 24th November – Mr Galbraith, of Folkestone, appeared in support of the summons. The prosecutor said that on last Tuesday week, November 24th, he was standing in his bar in the evening. He heard someone come in, and went to see who it was. He saw Thomas Dobson, the elder defendant, come in. Dobson never asked for any drink, so he ordered him off the premises. Defendant then caught hold of him by the collar of his coat. He tried to get away from him but could not. While in that position the other prisoner came in and struck him many times in his face. He managed to get into the tap room, and then the elder Dobson pulled him down by his collar, and the son kicked at him three or four times, and once kicked him on the eye while in that position. When he saw the blood running the younger defendant walked away.*

In reply to the elder prisoner, Joslin said when parties went to his shop to ask for bread he did not say "Don't go to that man's shop." He never struck him on the nose or scratched his neck. Sarah Joslin, - wife of prosecutor, corroborated.

Charles Smith, a lodger at the Military Tavern, and his Aunt, Mrs Joslin, called him, and when he came downstairs he saw his uncle bleeding very much, and saw the elder defendant being pulled away from the house.

The elder defendant said Joslin had been an annoyance for a long time past and had called his children bad names. He had reported prosecutor twice to the superintendent.

George Laming stated that on the evening in question he was just outside the Military Tavern. He saw the elder Dobson at the door of his house opposite to the tavern. Joslin was calling him most obscene names. Dobson went across to Joslin's house, and as soon as he went into the house, witness looked through the door and saw Joslin punching into him. Dobson was very drunk. The younger defendant went to get his father out and he could not, so a man named Green also went to the elder defence's assistance and took him across the road to his house.

Wallace Green said he heard Joslin swearing and calling one of the defendant's obscene names. The elder Dobson went across the road, and no sooner did he get into the public house, Joslin struck him several times. The younger defendant went across to help his father, and tried to get him away, but could not: therefore the witness went to Dobson's assistance. Joslin would not let Dobson go, so he caught hold of Dobson round the waist and snatched him away, and carried him across to his house.

The magistrates, having consulted in private, fined the elder defendant 10s, and 12s costs, and the younger defendant 10s and 5s costs, or fourteen days hard labour.'

Further down the road to Thomas' abode was the Eight Bells at number 43.

Over time this establishment had seen the usual number of complaints and issues with the local police and prosecution services. In 1846 three girls of the night had conspired steal some regimental items from a private in the 40th regiment. The girl, in whose room the items were found hidden under the mattress, was sent to prison for a fortnight for not paying a heavy fine. Five years before Thomas moved to King Street, the landlord of the pub, who had often appeared before the bench on matters of dispute with his wife, was brought up for an assault on a police constable. It seems the publican and his wife had been drinking and one of their many heated arguments had ensued during which the publican had hit his wife. The policeman on his nightly patrol at twelve thirty heard her calling 'murder' and begging him to come in to the pub to save her. The policeman hurried along the street watched by the neighbours who had been woken by the noise and were peering out of their windows to see the landlord's wife dripping with blood from a blow to her head. She begged the policeman to come in because her life was in danger. The policeman went in to arrest the landlord, who refused to go with him and ended up striking the policeman a severe blow on the head. The publican then tried to get three of the lodgers to help him, but they were frightened and blew out the candles and ran away. Some soldiers then arrived and tried to help, but the landlord bit two of them on the hand and ran to the bar where he armed himself with a shoemakers hammer and threatened to split open their heads. After a further scuffle the landlord was eventually collared and marched off to the police station, not before giving the policeman a severe and painful kick in the leg.

The landlord later claimed that his wife had started the scuffle by breaking his windows with stones, and calling out 'murder' which she was in the habit of doing. It seems that the wife had recently emerged from prison from acts of similar conduct herself. At his hearing the Mayor told the landlord that the Eight Bells was the worse conducted public house in the city and that he would definitely not have his licence renewed. He was fined the highest penalty of £5 and 6s in costs. The soldiers had to keep quiet, as they should not have been out of Barracks so late and would have been punished for doing so, but without their help the policeman could have received a much worse fate than a painful kick in the leg.

During the time that Thomas lived in King Street the Eight Bells was under new management, but still the police were called to the pub to deal with incidents of theft and drunkenness.

In 1867 a man was accused of stealing three bedspreads from the pub and leaving without paying for his lodging. He tried to sell the bedspreads before being caught and was sentenced to three months imprisonment.

In 1881 the landlord was fined the sum of 5s and 6d for being drunk in charge of a horse. He was also fined on two occasions that year for letting customers drink on the premises after hours.

In 1890 two live, tame rabbits valued at 8s and some goods and chattels were stolen from the landlord's wife, which resulted in the imprisonment for two months for the offender.

In 1891 the landlord was fined £2 for selling beers to two customers out of hours.

In 1905 the incumbent landlord became very ill. The doctor was called for and on seeing the patient declared that the man should be taken on a journey of eight miles to the Herne Bay Cottage hospital. Dr Bowes did not send the man off with a note of explanation. When the patient arrived at the Cottage hospital he was refused entry, as there was no accompanying note from the doctor. They claimed not have had a resident medical man on duty who could attend to unexpected cases. The Governors of the Cottage hospital considered they had been abused in this way in the past and had instructed the Matron not to admit patients without some kind of notice. On the night in question there had been three members of staff on duty- one nurse, the Matron and a probationer. The hapless patient then had to endure a tortuous eight mile journey back to Canterbury, where he subsequently died. An inquest was held into his death and in his summing up the Coroner remarked that he felt it was the duty of a medical man to see a case through, and not deal with it in that happy-go-lucky fashion. In his opinion the sick man should have stayed at home if there was no hope of his recovery where he should have been left to pass peacefully away. Canterbury did have a hospital at the time situated in Longport Street, but it had strict rules of entry and the admission of an ageing, dying man was not one of them.

In addition to being the focal meeting place of the street, public houses also formed Friendly Societies which were benefit clubs for the poor. Many of them also had Rat and Trap teams which competed with each other and were well supported by their regulars. Unfortunately, the downside of the profusion of local pubs meant that noisy brawls often ensued and it was clear that something had to be done to try and ease the situation. In an effort to lessen the evil of drink, magistrates declared that public houses should close at 10pm on Sundays and 11.30pm on weekdays.

Thomas' early experiences in the brickfields had exposed him to the effects of drink on hard working men, who were not above using verbal and physical means to stand up for themselves. In Canterbury he found many similarities between that life and the life of the Victorian poor of the city.

Chapter Six

The Family

Thomas lived in the parish of St. Alphage and his parish church was where all of his children were christened and then married. The church of St. Alphage was located in Palace Street, which was in the next street to the Dobson's home. It was built of flint and stone. The church was dedicated to an 11th century Archbishop of Canterbury who was captured by the Danes, who then demanded a huge ransom for his release. The Archbishop urged his countrymen not to pay the ransom and he was reputedly killed by the Danes throwing ox bones at him. The church also had links with some historical people. The man responsible for hiring the *Mayflower*, which took the Pilgrims to America in 1620, was married in the church and John Caxton, the brother of William Caxton who developed the printing press, is buried inside the church.

As Thomas' children grew and reached maturity, they inevitably started courting. For a woman to remain single was thought a disgrace and at thirty an unmarried woman was called an old maid. Lack of family planning meant that many couples found themselves with a baby already on the way when they got married.

Marriage laws of the time were based on the idea that women would get married and that their husbands would take care of them.

Once married, it was extremely difficult for a woman to obtain a divorce. Women had no legal right to a voice in deciding how their children were treated. The man of the house had all the control and the marriage ceremony included the obligatory wording that the woman would 'obey' her husband. In the 19th century British women were expected to marry and have children. Unfortunately this was also a time when women outnumbered men and so prospective husbands were in short supply. There were several reasons for this. The mortality rate was higher for boys than girls, many men served in the forces abroad and men were more likely to emigrate than women.

Thomas and Maria were both forty two when the first of their brood got married and what followed was a succession of marriages and the steady arrival of new grandchildren. The ups and downs of their children's lives meant that there was never a dull moment and their days were filled with the news of family life.

The first of Thomas' children to enter the state of matrimony was his eldest son, who married in 1882.

Frederick was seventeen when he started courting a servant girl by the name of Patience Brown. She had been born in the small village of Fordwich, just outside of the city. Her family then moved to London, but Patience later returned to Canterbury to work. She became another unmarried mother and, as soon as her pregnancy was noticed, Patience was immediately dismissed from her work. This was confirmed by the 1881 census which records her visiting family in Fordwich as a *'domestic servant - out of employ'*. However, Frederick married her on 24 December 1882 when they were both eighteen. They named their baby Priscilla. Frederick became a fish salesman and they settled into family life at 7, St Gregory's Place.

In March 1896 the East Kent Gazette reported that Frederick's wife, Patience, was accused of an assault on the head mistress of the infants' department of St. John's school. It seems the children had been late arriving at school and had been shut in the lavatory while the teacher was taking a religious instruction lesson. When Patience confronted the teacher as to why she had done this she replied *'I will not allow them to come in until I open the door.'* Patience was not happy with this, as she said her children should not be shut in the lavatory, which anyway was cold. At the end of the day Patience confronted the teacher again as she was walking home. Patience caught her by the nose and threatened to *'wring her nose out of her face.'* The caretaker was in her garden when she saw the couple shaking each other. A witness living in Broad Street stated that the teacher had abused Patience about her children and had commenced biting her. She then saw Patience strike the teacher on the side of the face. Following further investigations, it was found that children who were late for school were routinely shut out in the unheated lavatory, even on bitterly cold mornings, and this was not a school rule. The bench concluded that if Patience had any complaints as to the discipline of the school she ought to have appealed to the managers. She was fined 5s. and 14s.6d. costs.

Seven years later Frederick's job led to his father Thomas taking on an act of compassion and charity. Thomas took in a fourteen year old girl called Sarah Ann May, who is recorded as being '*adopted*' by him. Sarah was one of ten children born to a family living in a neighbouring street at 8, Knotts Lane in Staplegate. Sarah's father, John, had run a fishmonger and grocery store. The family were well known to the Dobson's and it is most likely that Frederick had been employed there as a fish salesman. On 25 September 1889 disaster struck the family when John died suddenly of a heart attack. His wife, Elizabeth, was so distraught that she died three days later on the 28 September. There was an inquest into her death at which an outcome of accidental death due to blood poisoning was recorded. It would seem that in her grief, the widow probably sought comfort through medication which unfortunately resulted in her death. All the orphaned children were farmed out to friends and family. Thomas took in Sarah who was the same age as his daughter Elizabeth and probably went to school with her. Sarah lived with Thomas until she went into service. By the age of twenty two she was working as a domestic stillroom maid at the County Hotel in the High Street.

Thomas' mother had been living with him for some seventeen years and her health was gradually deteriorating. For some time she had been suffering from valvular disease of the heart. She suffered shortness of breath, chest pain, fatigue and dizziness. Despite her condition, Elizabeth still made the occasional visit out. On the 11 March 1887, when she was seventy four years of age, she made a visit to nearby friends and family living at 22 Artillery Street. It was while she was there that she fell into a faint and suffered a fatal heart attack. Thomas was shocked and saddened by this news, but comforted to know that his mother had enjoyed a life at the heart of two families and lived long enough to see one of her grandchildren married.

Two years later it was time for two more of Thomas's children to get married.

Annie Marie married at the age of twenty one in 1889. Annie had been courted by John Parry, who lived next to the Dobson's at 33 King Street. He was a leather seller's assistant. Annie Marie was a music teacher. In the nineteenth century there was a 'flood' of private music teachers in the expanding market and for this reason it had a reputation as a low-status part of the profession. This couple set up home at 24, Hospital Lane, where John became a traveller for the leather tannery. They later moved to 44, Stour Street when John had progressed to the role of Foreman in the company. The couple had seven children.

William also married in 1889. He married Clara Frances Stroud, who was a dressmaker. Tragically Clara died just six months after the wedding. A year later, on 26 December 1890, the twenty three year old widower remarried. His second wife was Annie Johnson Lee who was born in Dover. William started married life living with his brother Thomas junior and his wife. Both brothers were bakers like their father. William's wife wanted to return to Dover and so he found a position in that town as a licensed victualler at 50, St James Lane. The couple had six children.

Two more years passed until in 1891, when Thomas and Maria turned fifty, it was the turn of his namesake to get married.

Thomas junior was twenty four and a baker when he married the pregnant Adeline Tilly. Her father ran the Two Bells Public House in Military Road, where Adeline worked as a barmaid. They started their married life with Thomas' brother William at 21, Havelock Street. Their first child, William Thomas Frank was born months after their wedding. The couple went on to have two more children. They eventually took over the running of the Two Bells with Thomas jnr. and his son William doing the baking and Adeline running the pub.

The Two Bells at 59 Military Road was a well known establishment at the time. In the early days it was often used as a place to hold local inquests.

In 1843 the inquest involved the death of a soldier from the Barracks. A Private in the 7th Hussars was on stable duty when he was kicked in the arm and stomach by his grey mare. He was taken to the Military hospital where he died of his injuries. A verdict of accidental death was recorded, but it was suggested the mare should be put down.

In 1862 an inquest was held into the sad case of the discovery of the dead body of a child found in St. Gregory's Cemetery. The sexton gave the following statement which was recorded in the Kentish Chronicle. 11 January. 1862

'I inter, without burial service, the bodies of still-born children in the churchyard. I have recently interred some such bodies- as many as five bodies of still-born children in the churchyard. I have recently interred some such bodies- as many as four in the last fortnight. I receive no certificate to state that they are still-born. It was not necessary. On Sunday last, at three o'clock in the afternoon, I was in the churchyard looking for a place for a grave, when I observed that a recently made grave had been disturbed. I had my shovel in my hand, and was about to remake the grave, but the shovel struck against something, which proved to be a coffin. It had not been placed there by me, and I know nothing about it. I gave information on Sunday morning to the police. On that morning the coffin was opened in my presence, and the body of a female child was discovered.'

The coroner and jury concluded that the sextant acted improperly and illegally in burying children without a certificate, whether they were still-born or not. The post mortem revealed that the baby had indeed been still-born. The coffin had been well made and lined. An initialled napkin had been wrapped around the body, but, despite all efforts, the discovery of the person who placed the coffin there had not been found.

In 1864 the landlord was charged with selling beer at the new quarters for married soldiers at the Barracks.

In 1870 an inquest was held into another body of a female infant found in St Gregory's churchyard. In this case the body of the child was found lying near the wall.

'Mr. Holttum, surgeon, said he believed the deceased was not attended in her confinement by a medical man, the umbilical cord not having been tied. From its size and general appearance he believed the child was born alive.'

The jury, however, returned a verdict of 'Still-born.'

Whitstable Times and Herne Bay Herald, 12 February 1870

Later that year a discharged soldier was charged with assaulting the landlord of the pub by striking him on the face during an altercation.

In addition to running the Two Bells, Thomas jnr. also ran a bakery and confectioners shop at 21 Havelock Street. He hired Mary

Parren to manage the shop and to look after his two young boys while he was working in the public house.

On the 19 October 1901 the following article appeared in the Canterbury Journal.

'DID NOT WEIGH THE LOAF. Thomas Dobson of Havelock Street, was summoned for selling bread otherwise than by weight on September 28th. Defendant pleaded guilty.

It appeared that Sergeant Swain sent a little boy into defendant's shop for a loaf, which was served to him without being weighed. When Sergeant Swain went to the shop and had the loaf weighed it was found to be 1 ½ oz short of two pounds.

Defendant said in his housekeeper's absence from the shop his little boy, aged ten, served the customer, although he had been told not to do it. He (defendant) always sold bread by weight.

The Bench imposed a fine of 2s. 6d and 10s. 6d costs. Superintendent Farmery called the attention of the magistrates to the fact that very light penalties were inflicted at that Court for offences under the Weights and Measures Act, some of which were very bad cases. The Mayor said the Magistrates dealt with each case on its merits.'

In 1897 when the couple reached the age of fifty seven, it was the turn of their fifth child to get married.

Arthur, aged twenty three, married Jane Whenman in 1897. Jane was the daughter of a soldier. As a child she was living in the Brompton Barracks in the school of Military Engineering in Gillingham, while her father was on active duty. He was a company Sergeant Major. Her mother died when she was eleven and her father took his family to Bloomsbury in London where he died the year after Jane married Arthur. Arthur and Jane moved to Fordwich near Canterbury where they ran the Fordwich Arms Public House, next to the river Stour. They had four children. In 1903 they moved to the Three Cups public House at 18 Broad Street, but sadly after three years Jane died. Arthur found himself left with four children, the youngest of whom was only two years old. Arthur moved to 15 Victoria Avenue in Margate where he worked as a baker and the four children went to school. He hired a young housekeeper, named Rose to help with the children. Rose was ten years his junior. In providing a reference for Arthur when he was called up to military service in 1914, the landlord of his house wrote the following testimony-

'I have known Arthur Edward Dobson of 15 Victoria Avenue, Margate for some years. Also Rose Violet Bolton for about two years who has been a good and faithful housekeeper to both him and his family. I have found them quiet, orderly people and good t

John Miles 6 Nov 1914.

In time Rose became more than a housekeeper and the couple had two children together. Rose considered herself married, although no legal ceremony ever took place. She did eventually get married to Arthur Wilton when she was fifty years of age.

In 1918 Arthur's daughter, Elsie Mary, died at the age of thirteen. She died at home of heart failure following a bout of diphtheria and similar complications. This crippling disease, caused by bacterial infection, was known as *'the Strangling Angel of Childhood'*, as it was a particular threat to young children. Arthur was serving in France at the time of Elsie's death and was granted sick leave from the army at this time of grief.

The next five years were quiet ones for Thomas and it was not until he reached the age of sixty two, that his second daughter married.

Elizabeth Mary married Walter George Bates in 1902 when she was 23 years old. George was boarding with her family at 30 King Street and he worked as a leather cutter. Her brothers, Thomas jnr. and William, were witnesses at their sister's wedding. The couple set up home nearby at 9, The Borough, where they ran a tobacconist shop. Seven years later they had a son named Walter George after his father. Elizabeth found herself a widow by the age of thirty one when her husband was found dead in the River Stour. Walter's body was identified by her brother Thomas jnr. The inquest into the death recorded a verdict of natural causes.

Elizabeth Bates/ nee Dobson

Two years later, in 1913, Elizabeth married Frederick George Chapman, who was a soldier in the Royal Engineers 3rd Field Troop in Canterbury Barracks where he was a shoe smith. Elizabeth was close to her brother Thomas jnr. and his wife Adeline Tilley and the couple were witnesses to her second wedding in St. Alphage church. At the time of the marriage, Elizabeth was living at 20 Lion Cottages and Frederick was in the Barracks. Following their marriage, the couple moved to 57 Broad Street which was the property and married quarters of the Barracks. Frederick served in WW1 between 1914 and 1920. Elizabeth had a second son, named Frederick after his father, and her two boys grew up together. When her husband left the army in 1920, the couple moved to the Butchers Arms public house in Butchery Lane where they became the licensed victuallers. They lived there until 1926 when Elizabeth became a widow for the second time.

For a short while she ran the Ben Johnson public house in the main high street, which was reportedly the smallest pub in Canterbury. From there Elizabeth became the publican of the Wincheap Arms where she lived with her two sons until they, in turn, left home to get married. Following this she lived alone and ran the pub single handed with some weekend help from her second son who lived nearby and whom she went to live with at the end of her life. Elizabeth died aged seventy seven of a burst appendix in the Nunnery Field hospital.

Elizabeth Bates Chapman/nee Dobson (left) with a friend.

Another two years passed and Thomas had reached the age of sixty four years old by the time his next son married in 1904.

Percival fathered a child when he was seventeen. It is not known what happened to the mother, but Thomas senior and Maria took in the child, who was named Ethel, and she and her father continued to live in the family home. When Percy eventually got married, his daughter Ethel was ten years old. In later life, Ethel's cousin Maria, the daughter of her Uncle Frederick, moved to Gillingham to marry James Carter. Ethel then married James's younger brother, Percy Carter and also moved to Gillingham to live. Ethel had three children, but died in 1909 when she was just twenty five years old.

Percy married Henrietta Frost in 1904 in Dover, where she was born, and their daughter, Ivy, was born nine months later. Henrietta's father was a wheelwright and she trained as a draper and milliner. The couple went on to have three boys. By 1911 the couple had rented a house at 21, Eva Road in Gillingham where Henrietta lived with the four children. Percy was not living with them, but was a boarder at number 300, Canterbury Road in Gillingham. The head of that house was a baker, confectioner and caterer. He had four married bakers boarding in the house without their families. The bakery business demanded long hours with little time for sleep and in this way the business owner was able to set the hours the men were available for work. The bakers would have worked at the back of the shop in their white coats and caps. Every so often they would have appeared from the back room with a tray of hot bread on their head. The tasty, white crusty loaves would have smelled wonderful. Once Percy achieved the status of Master Baker, the family moved back to

Dover where they had two more sons. Henrietta died in 1933 at the age of fifty three. Percy continued to live with his two sons, Percival junior and William, at 48 Military Road. All three of them were Master Bakers and very well known in the area.

Percival's wife Henrietta Frost.

In 1906 it was the turn of the last of the children to marry. Thomas and Maria were now sixty six and must have thought that they could now look forward to a peaceful old age. Unfortunately that was not to be as storm clouds would soon be brewing.

Frank By the age of fifteen Frank was working as a grocer's assistant in a shop at 63/64 Union Street. As a boy of fourteen he was called to give witness in a case where a small child had been run over by a man driving a grey cob with a four wheel van loaded behind. The man was accused of driving at a dangerous rate. The paper recorded that the child did not move until the wheel moved, so thankfully it does not seem to have been a fatal accident, but the extent of any injuries are not recorded. Frank stated that;

'On Saturday the 14th of this month he was near Mr. Callow's shop about four o'clock. He saw the defendant driving a horse attached to a van steadily. He was not using a whip.'

At the age of twenty Frank married Mary Jessie Mills. Mary's father was a general grocer at 23 Military Road. The couple's daughter, Eva, was born nine months later. Their first years of marriage were spent at 1 Mill Lane.

Frank's wife   Mary Jessie Mills

Their daughter, Eva Jessie, married a soldier from the Military Barracks called Harry Herbet Latus in 1918 when she was twenty one. Eva gave birth to a son nine months later. Unfortunately it turned out that the dashing cavalry man in the Yorkshire Dragoons was already married and therefore a bigamist. Eva's illegitimate son was called Bobbie and he died aged twenty in the battle of Dunkirk in 1920. Harry Latus and his legal wife had two children who were born in Hull. He was sentenced at York Assizes on 26 June 1923 to nine month's hard labour for bigamy. Eva remarried Albert Ralph in Oct 1923 under her maiden name. The couple lived in Maidstone.

Thomas and Maria were a devoted couple. They both worked hard to provide and care for their large family. All eight of their children's weddings would have been small, family affairs with the brides wearing serviceable clothes, which were practical for reuse. The colourful lives of their children and some forty grandchildren meant that life for Thomas and Maria was never going to be dull.

Chapter Seven

Old Age

Throughout all the many comings and goings of his large family, Thomas remained a constant provider and supporter of his wife Maria. They had lived together in their house at 30 King Street, Canterbury all their married life and knew many people in the area. However, as old age approached, change was about to happen.

Thomas had worked long and unsociable hours as a Master Baker all his adult life. It was not until he was nearly seventy that Thomas was finally able to slow down and retire. The first Old Age Pension Act of 1908 finally came into being on 1st January 1909. The pension was means tested for the very poorest of *good character* aged seventy and over. The amount of pension money given was kept deliberately low to encourage people to continue working. A married couple received a shared payment of seven shillings and six pence a week.

Due to the nature of his work, Thomas found himself eligible for charitable housing. Almshouses allocated under this scheme were often known as *bedeshouses* and the occupants as *bedesmen and bedeswomen*. In earlier times bedesmen were employed by the church to pray for the souls of the departed. Thomas and Maria were provided with a little, terraced bedeshouse backing on to the River

Stour by the Westgate at 5 Pound Lane. The street was so called because of the city pound which was located at number 1. This was originally where stray animals were put to be claimed, for a fee, by their owners. The building was later used as a goal and by 1829 an early police station had been erected on this site.

In October 1909, when Thomas and Maria may well have just moved house, Pound Lane was flooded following a bout of torrential rain. Four inches of rain fell over the course of three days and many streets were impassable. Wooden planks were erected outside of houses to allow some pedestrian access. Transport at the time was by bicycle or horse and carriage. The delivery of daily milk supplies was important and horse drawn milk carts continued to struggle through the rising water. One postman delivered mail from a boat to people in their bedrooms via the use of a long pole.

In 1914 the unthinkable happened when Britain was drawn into a world war. As Thomas lived in a garrison town and very close to the Barracks, he was accustomed to seeing soldiers walking and riding horses around the city. The Royal Cavalry Barracks was the head quarters of all the cavalry regiments on Foreign Service and ensured that horses and mounted soldiers were a feature of everyday life on the streets. The foot soldiers were always to be seen, in shops and public houses, during parades and at important civil celebrations. When troops were sent off on manoeuvres to foreign parts, Thomas was used to seeing crowds of people lining the streets to cheer them on their way.

A life in service attracted many, but in the 1850's, following the Crimean war against Russia, serious weaknesses in the size of the army had been revealed. At that time the terms of service required men to serve for periods of twenty one years and this put many men off enlisting. In 1859 the War Office decided that the army should be supplemented by a part time volunteer force. In 1870 Parliament passed the Army Enlistment Act. Men could now sign on for a maximum of twelve years, but serve usually six months with the regular army and the remainder of the time only as part-time training, but with a commitment to serve up if called up at a time of war. The beginning of WW1 highlighted the urgent need for more men to fight and compulsory call up was introduced for all single men between the ages of eighteen and forty one. This was later amended to include married men and the age increased to fifty one. Those exempt from call up were those medically unfit, clergymen, teachers, widowers with young children and certain classes of industrial workers.

The East Kent division of the Buffs was one of the oldest regiments of the army, dating back to 1572. In 1914 a new branch was raised in Canterbury and housed in the Howe Barracks as part of Kitchener's Third New Army and this is where most of the Dobson men were recruited. Of Thomas' seven sons the youngest three were required to serve, as were some of his grandsons. Like everyone else in the country who was wracked with worry about family members, this was a devastating time for Thomas and Maria, who were now aged seventy four and beginning to suffer from ill health. Thomas would have known that his youngest sons and eldest grandsons had been called up to serve in the war, but, unlike his poor wife, he did not live long enough to see any of them killed.

In 1917 Thomas's life turned full circle. His health gradually deteriorated to such an extent that he was unable to care for himself and he was sent to the workhouse infirmary. This workhouse had been erected in Nunnery Fields between 1848 and 1850 to house around 400 inmates. In 1883 a 70 bed infirmary block was built to the west of the workhouse and this is where the sick and old people of Canterbury were sent who could no longer care for themselves.

The New Canterbury Workhouse Nunnery Fields 1849

Obviously Maria, who was also eighty, would have been distressed to see Thomas taken into the workhouse, but she was clearly unable to care for him herself. The term 'senile decay' was used loosely at the time, but refers to the progressive loss of mental capacity that leads to dementia and personal helplessness. In the majority of cases recorded at the time, this most likely referred to Alzheimer's disease. Thomas died on the 7th February 1917 at the age of seventy seven. His death certificate records his cause of death as senile decay and was registered by the Master of the Workhouse.

Thomas was buried in the Canterbury City Cemetery in Westgate Court Avenue in grave number seventy five.

Maria survived Thomas by another ten years. She left the house in Pound Lane and went to live with her youngest daughter in the Butchers Arms at 10 Butchery Lane.

The Butchers Arms. Butchery Lane

Maria spent her last years with her daughter Elizabeth, her son in law and her two grandsons, Percy Bates and Fred Chapman, until she became very frail and unwell. At this point Maria was also admitted into the Workhouse Infirmary where Thomas had died, although by now it had the more pleasing title of 'The Home.' On the 19th May 1927, when she was nearly eighty seven, Maria died of senile gangrene. This term referred to a lack of blood supply, mainly to the extremities. Her death was registered by her son Percy Dobson who lived in Dover.

Maria was buried with her beloved husband Thomas in the Canterbury cemetery.

Endnote

WW1 records for Thomas' family.

<u>Sons</u>

Arthur, service number S/29802, whose Royal Army Service for the Buffs East Kent Regiment papers inform us that, at the age of nearly thirty eight, he was five feet eight inches tall, ten and a half pounds in weight, with light brown hair and grey eyes and a scar over his right eye. Arthur signed up in November 1814 in Margate. He was enlisted to the Supply department, as he was a cook and baker. An army marches on its stomach and Arthur's skills were needed in the field bakery. He went on to serve in India and South Africa. He became a sergeant and his discharge papers record that:

'He is a very good and willing worker and a capable H.P.C. with good control of men. He is willing, honest, sober and reliable and gave satisfaction.'

Arthur was admitted to hospital as a casualty and discharged from the army in 1820 after six years and fifty eight days service.

Frank, service number 9208, served with the Buffs East Kent Regiment. He was listed as wounded on the Casualty list issued by the War Office from 19/02/1915. He was entitled to wear a 'Wound Stripe' as authorised under Army Order 204 of 6th July 1916.

Percival survived WW1 because he was a Master Baker and his services were needed to feed the people in this country. However, he was not so lucky in WW2, when the Second World War resulted in bombing raids on Dover in 1941. Percy became a civilian casualty. He survived his injuries and was taken to the Preston Hall Hospital in Aylesford, near Maidstone, where he died eleven days later of his injuries. His funeral received coverage in the Dover Express which records that on the day his service was attended by his six children, his sister Elizabeth Chapman and her daughters in law, Mrs Percival Bates and Mrs Frederick Chapman who were his nieces.

Grandchildren

Charles, (son of Frederick) service number G/13300 was a bandsman in the Buffs. He was killed in action in Flanders on 24 June 1917 aged thirty.

William, (son of Thomas jnr.) Service number T/265244 was a corporal in the 1st Battalion of the Buffs. He was killed in action in Flanders on 23 March 1918 aged twenty nine. He was a Master Baker.

The records for these deaths are kept in the Buffs East Kent Regt. Book of Remembrance in the Warrior Chapel of Canterbury Cathedral. Each weekday at eleven a.m. the bell of HMS Canterbury is rung and a page in one of the Books of Life is turned.

Canterbury Cemetery Records

The following members of the Dobson family are buried in the city cemetery at Westgate Court Avenue. They are all to be found in **Section D** of the graveyard.

Thomas and Maria Ann .... grave number 75.

Frederick and Patience ....grave number 76.

Jane Whenman (wife of Arthur)............................. grave number 40.

Thomas jnr. and Adeline ....grave number 29.

Elizabeth Bates/Chapman (nee Dobson) ....grave number 2C.

Section S

Annie Maria Parry (nee Dobson)............................grave number 653.

Plan of Canterbury Cemetery

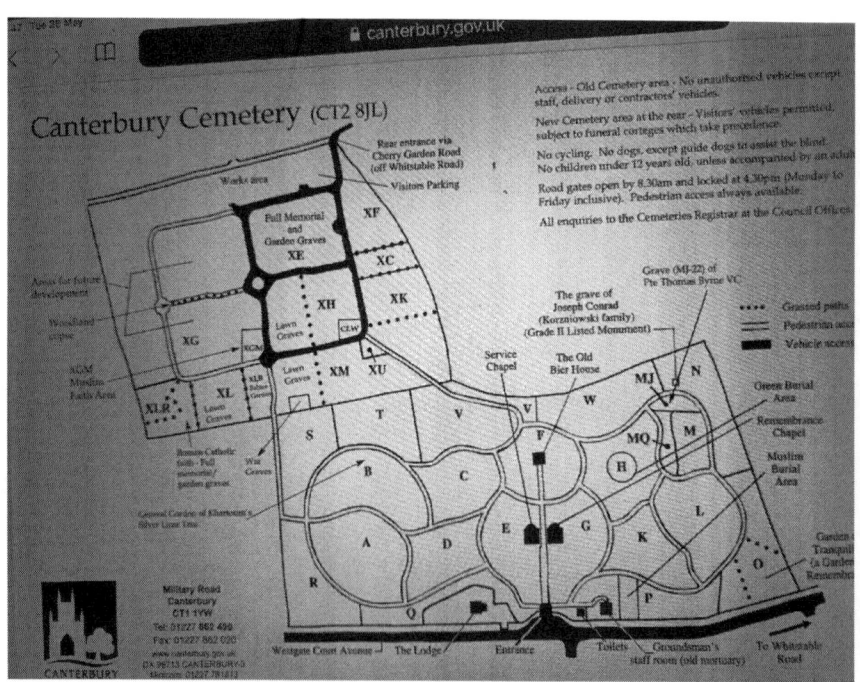

References and Acknowledgements

Canterbury Journal

Canterbury Farmers Gazette

East Kent Gazette

Faversham Union Workhouse by John Stevens

Kentish Gazette

Kentish Chronicle

Photograph of Thomas and Maria supplied by Margaret Hart

Photographs of Elizabeth Dobson supplied by Margaret Hart

Photographs of Henrietta and Jessie supplied by Colin Dobson.

Photographs of the Butchers Arms and the Military Tavern by Rory Kehoe

Picture of HMS Waterloo from Wikipedia

Prints of Canterbury Cathedral and Workhouse from Victorian Canterbury by Audrey Bateman

Whitstable and Herne Bay Herald.

Victorian Canterbury by Audrey Bateman 1991   ISBN 0 86023 477 0

Postscript

From humble beginnings in a workhouse, Thomas Dobson went on to live a long, productive and colourful life. His typical Victorian, working class roots meant that he knew hardship and had developed a tough exterior. Like most men of his time, he enjoyed a drink and on occasions was known to drink to excess. However, Thomas was proud of his family. Through his example of becoming a Master Baker, at least three of his sons followed him to become bakers in their own right. Although he did not have a close relationship with his mother in the early years, they kept in contact and became close when his mother was widowed and went to live with him in her later life.

Thomas started life in the confines of a workhouse and ended his life in a workhouse. Between these years he successfully made his way in life and there are many relatives alive today who owe him a great debt of gratitude for his time on this earth.

Printed in Great Britain
by Amazon